SYNTHESIS SERIES

To whom shall we go?

Christ and the mystery of man

FRANCISCAN HERALD PRESS
1434 West 51st St. • Chicago, Ill. 60609

To whom shall we go by Zachary Hayes O.F.M. Copyright ©1975 by Franciscan Herald Press, 1434 West 51st Street, Chicago, Illinois 60609. Made in the United States of America.

ISBN 0-8199-0702-2

NIHIL OBSTAT:
Mark Hegener O.F.M.
Censor

IMPRIMATUR:
Msgr. Richard Rosemeyer J.D.
Vicar General, Archdiocese of Chicago

October 10, 1975

"The Nihil Obstat and the Imprimatur are official declarations that a book or pamphlet is free of doctrinal or moral error. No implication is contained therein that those who have granted the Nihil Obstat and Imprimatur agree with the contents, opinions or statements expressed."

CONTENTS

INTRODUCTION 7

CHAPTER I
Jesus without Dogma? 11

CHAPTER II
The Person and the Image 21

CHAPTER III
The Story of Jesus 30

CHAPTER IV
Put to Death for our Sins 39

CHAPTER V
Raised for our Justification 52

CONCLUSION 62

EDITORIAL PREFACE

THE AIM OF SYNTHESIS SERIES

As the growing edge of knowledge increases its pace and widens the domain of man, new vistas strike us which are both exciting and frightening. Although the spreading light reveals more and more the marvels of our universe, still the bordering darkness of the unknown expands along with it.

Nowhere is the uncharted field of the universe of being more deeply felt today than in the area which concerns man himself. Here especially our growing knowledge deepens awareness of the vast unknown beyond our present range of vision.

We have begun to realize that the project of comprehending man is indeed gigantic. It is the conviction of all who seriously contemplate the problem that only a multi-disciplinary approach and synthesis will produce a true picture. We find emerging a cooperative effort by those engaged in any discipline which bears upon understanding man and promoting his well-being. The human sciences, the arts, philosophy, religion and all the helping arts reveal him in the several dimensions of his complex pattern of life.

SYNTHESIS SERIES is intended to introduce the reader to the experience of using the multi-disciplinary approach when attempting to understand himself and others. We believe this will lead to his perceiving and relating to the entire human family more effectively — that is, more in accord with rich depth and breadth of all those realities it contains. We hope this will help reduce the confusion caused by the over-simplified "answers" to problems of living which used to be offered by specialists in various fields.

Instead of the easy or quick answers we propose that each individual make steady serious effort to achieve a rich synthesis of concepts developed by many disciplines. This appears to be the only method that holds the promise of yielding the fundamental answer — the meaning his own existence is supposed to have — a meaning so often fretfully and falteringly sought by everyone whether he admits it or not. The promise and its realization in personal experience provide sufficient motive to undertake and sustain the search. But beyond this, one can foresee benefits which transcend individual well-being. For personal growth of many individuals brings about a **social atmosphere** which stimulates still further development toward a more meaningful life on the part of each member of the group.

This interaction between an individual and others is apparent when we observe the opposite process of deterioration. Just as the most disruptive factor in society is the unrest caused by failure of its members to find the meaning of life, so the reverse holds true, that society will benefit at all levels in proportion to the success people have in their quest for the meaning they believe their existence is supposed to have.

SYNTHESIS SERIES, we repeat, is intended to introduce the reader to the new multi-disciplinary method in carrying out the search for the meaning his life is to have when viewed in reference to the destiny of mankind.

INTRODUCTION

During the years since the promulgation of the documents of Vatican II, the interest of the Church throughout the world has been focused largely on questions of ecclesiology: on the renewal of Christian life and the renovation of structures. Given the circumstances, this was understandable and perhaps inevitable. Yet with the passing of time, it has become increasingly clear that the issues we have tried to deal with at the level of structure, worship, and ministry cannot be handled adequately without raising fundamental issues in the area of Christology.

Many specialized studies in Christology have appeared in recent years, but in general these are available only to those who read professional theological journals or highly technical theological literature. Yet much of this material is beyond the stage of mere probing and can now be assessed as solid theological theory. This is material which would provide an image of Christ that takes into account the well-documented findings of Scripture scholars and historians. Such an image, as it is now beginning to emerge, would be of great benefit to many Christians for whom the handbook presentation has lost much of its former power. For many Christians, the theological style of presenting the mystery of Christ has led to a situation in which Christ is virtually devoid of human meaning. Yet it has been the mission of the Church from the beginning to indicate how the person and destiny of Jesus is for the sake of mankind. If he is truly for mankind, his mystery must be laden with profound human meaning for men of every age.

Part of the present problem relates to the fact that Christological teaching tends to be almost one-sidedly objective and spends little time developing the human significance of what is said. The meaning of Jesus for mankind is generally dealt with simply in terms of the classical doctrine of vicarious satisfaction which is indeed limited, and, to many contemporary Christians, is unconvincing. In dealing with the person of Christ himself, we have gradually narrowed the riches of tradition into a very small but persistent channel namely: the Scholastic theory on the psychological constitution of Christ. This theory has become virtually normative for catechesis and preaching, and yet it is laden with problems which ought not to be confused with matters of faith. Since Christians, to a great extent, have lost a sense of the audacious claims the Christian community has come to make about one who appeared within history as a fellow man, it would be healthy to recover some sense of the historical route by which the community emerged and thus learn to appreciate why St. Paul could refer to Christ as both a scandal and a stumbling block. The Christian claims about Christ, while profound in their meaning, are neither obvious nor self-evident. The historical approach to the origins of our Faith is a great aid in recovering a true sense of the unique qualities of Christianity.

The range of topics covered in this booklet is intentionally very limited. Our purpose is not to present a history of Christology, nor to cover all aspects of Christology, but rather to focus on the place of Christology in the life of the Church, and above all on those mysteries from which Christology takes its origin; namely, on the life, death, and Resurrection of Jesus Christ. A more critical awareness concerning these issues will help greatly to avoid mythological understandings of the Church's Faith and will clear the ground for a more mature understanding of the later dogma of Chalcedon. The task of constructing a full systematic Christology remains to be done. In the mean time, it is our hope to fill a gap in the current, popular literature by making available to a wider reading public some key insights of contemporary theology bearing on the basic mystery of the Christian Faith.

It is the intent of the present reflections to present some of the best and well-established insights concerning the person and work of Christ in a non-technical format. The author makes no claim to originality. Rather, he works on the assumption that truth is a public possession; and, following the spirit of medieval scholars, he draws freely from the hard-won insights of other theologians where their work seems well-established. Since our intent is not to offer a work that is critical and scientific in its own right, but to present material that has been critically established already, we will forego the use of extensive documentation. In as far as possible, we will recognize the authors from whom many of these insights are gleaned, but will generally omit specific citations to their works. This procedure has recommended itself largely for the sake of simplifying the format of the text.

Among the most influential writers to whom the present author owes a great debt in arriving at his personal assessment of many Christological issues are the following:

> R. Fuller, *The Foundations of New Testament Christology* (Scribner, 1965).
>
> Van Harvey, *The Historian and the Believer,* (Macmillan, 1966).
>
> W. Kasper, *Jesus der Christus,* (Grünewald, 1974).
>
> W. Pannenberg, *Jesus, God and Man,* (Westminster, 1968).
>
> K. Rahner, *On the Theology of Death,* Quaes. disp. 2, (Herder and Herder, 1965).
>
> ———, "Resurrection," *Sacramentum mundi* 5 (Herder and Herder, 1970).
>
> J. Ratzinger, *Introduction to Christianity,* (Herder and Herder, 1970).
>
> B. Vawter, *This Man Jesus: An Essay toward a New Testament Christology* (Doubleday, 1973).

Whenever direct reference is made to any of these, we will indicate in parentheses only the name of the author and the pertinent pages.

> REV. ZACHARY HAYES, O.F.M.
> *Catholic Theological Union*
> Chicago, Ill.

Chapter I
JESUS WITHOUT DOGMA?

It is clear that the preaching of the Church is not simply identical with that of Jesus of Nazareth. Many today who have problems with the Church and yet seem concerned with Jesus tend to by-pass the Church and its dogmas by a direct appeal to the simple gospel of the historical Jesus. For some the dogma of the Church appears to be an unnecessary complication of something that is at root very simple, while for others dogma is rejected as an outright corruption of the gospel.

Impatience with dogma is found among many young people who, in all sincerity, attempt to do the impossible, namely: to answer the question of the meaning of Jesus for themselves with no reference to tradition, or even to the present Church-community. Here Jesus is often reduced to the figure of a gentle preacher of the ethic of love and universal brotherhood, much in the style of Harnack. Frequently He is seen as a model of ethical behavior not really different from other noble human persons. It has even been suggested that for those who find it difficult or impossible to say that they believe in God, it is possible to have a Jesus without God, and to find in him the source of our understanding of human life.

Most current popular movements focus on

Jesus in fundamentalist terms and seek to by-pass the Church so as to come directly to the real Jesus in Scripture. Spokesmen of such movements seem to think that it is enough to say "Jesus is God" or "Jesus is my personal Savior" without asking how one comes to say this or what it could possibly mean. Part of the enthusiasm seems to come from the discovery of Jesus as a fellow human being, as a brother, as the model of the simple, good life. And around the simple Jesus has grown a style of pop-art in which Jesus is clothed with the robes of a folk-hero. In all this, there is no room for the complications of exegesis or historical studies, and precious little room for the Church.

More self-conscious in its rejection of Christological dogma is the work of certain theologians as the impact of historical studies began to make itself felt in Christian circles. In terms of the historical-critical method, the question is unavoidable as to whether the Gospel descriptions of the earthly Jesus can be taken as accurate at any level. Has the account of his life been so modified by the Easter experience that it is no longer possible to discern the historical reality of Jesus himself? It has been suggested that Jesus never existed as an historical personage; that either he or his disciples were fraudulent deceivers; that he is the symbol of perfect humanity created by the collective consciousness of the community; that he was a man outstanding for the purity of his religious experience; that he was a religious enthusiast suffering from an inflated self-image;

that he was a religious fanatic who seemed always to hear the trumpets of the Last Judgment.

Diverse as these may seem, one thing they have in common, namely: the conviction that there is a fundamental separation between Jesus and his preaching on the one hand, and the Church with its preaching on the other. Not only is there a separation, but that which the Church has come to preach about Jesus from the early New Testament Christologies up to and including the dogma of Chalcedon appears to be a fundamental corruption of the original meaning of Jesus. That step whereby the Christian community placed Jesus in the center of its confession was, they say, the fatal mistake.

But now, the hope of the scholars was that more adequate tools of scientific, historical research would enable them to correct the error. "Back to the Jesus of history" was the program; back by means of a methodology that would explode the pervasive hold which the dogma of the traditional creed had gained in the Church. An objective picture of the historical Jesus, freed of the encrustations of community interpretations, was what they proposed; yet in the final analysis, each of these authors created a "real Jesus" in accord with his own tastes and preferences. That which they called the "Jesus of history" turned out to be an artificial construct rather than a picture of the actual Jesus who walked the roads of Palestine. Little wonder that a strong reaction should set in, for such an understanding of the Jesus of history seemed to have little if any significance for the Faith of the Christian community.

Thus the way was prepared for the work of Bultmann. On the one hand, the search for the historical Jesus seemed to be truly a dead-end street. On the other hand, the parallels between Christianity and the myths of other religious systems seemed too obvious to be denied. Strongly influenced by Bousset, Bultmann could come to say that Jesus conceived of himself neither as a bringer of salvation nor as one sent with a divine mission. Rather, he was concerned with calling to mind the character of decision in each present moment of human life. He was a noble man who died a tragic death.

As his followers came to see in his death the conquest of egotistic and materialistic forces destructive of human life, the kerygma emerged, namely: the proclamation of the saving-meaning of Jesus. And from this emerged the Gospels with all the mythological symbolism whereby early Christians sought to give expression to their conviction. The Resurrection of Jesus is the rise of a new consciousness in the disciples. What is important for us, they say, is not any information about the historical personage of Jesus; but a response of faith to the kerygma: the Christ-of-faith. Certainly in Bultmann's view such a man as Jesus actually lived; but his ministry and teaching belong to the Old Testament and not to the New. There is no intrinsic relation between the teaching of Jesus and the preaching of the Church. Thus, we arrive at the paradoxical situation in which, while the kerygma is a call to a new style of existence, there is no intrinsic relation between the kerygma and the quality of life by which it came into the world. There seems to be no real reason why it is linked with Jesus rather than with some other historical figure.

From a variety of starting points, therefore, the figure of Jesus appears as nothing more than a man. He is not to be taken as the content of religion, but at best as a perfect, religious man, or as the man who awakened the true religious sense in others. Christological dogma, from the very start, if it is understood to be a statement about the reality of Jesus, is seen as a fatal misunderstanding of the original intentions of Jesus.

The question of the Christological dogma may be seen to involve several levels. One that appears most clearly is that of the relation between the councils of the early Church and the writings of the New Testament. But historical studies lead unavoidably to the further question of the origins of Christology in the New Testament itself. Does the New Testament Christology have any positive relation to the person and work of Jesus; or is it totally and exclusively the creation of the community? The latter question will be discussed first, since the answer to that will determine whether there is any point to asking the first question.

Where does New Testament Christology begin? This question is raised by the fact that, not only does Chalcedon produce a faith-formula found nowhere in the New Testament, but it seems beyond reasonable doubt that even the earliest faith-confessions of the New Testament are not a simple continuation of the preaching of Jesus. The difference is stated in an overly simple form by Harnack when he says that Jesus proclaimed the Father while the Church proclaims the Son. The fact seems incontrovertible that the preaching of the Church is not simply identical with that of Jesus. Does the Christian faith, then, really derive from a divine revelation in Jesus, or is it exclusively the creation of the disciples? What is at issue here is the very essence of the Christian faith; for if there is no positive and intrinsic connection between the person of Jesus and the preaching of the Church, between Jesus and the Christ, then the only object which Christian proclamation has ever had would be destroyed. Is Christology an expression of the truth about the historical Jesus? For if the pre-Easter Jesus was only a man who proclaimed a message that had nothing to do with his own person and death, then the post-Easter faith would be nothing more than a religious idea which had come to be projected back to Jesus by chance. And if Easter is not in some sense the legitimation of the claim implicit in Jesus' mission, then it is nothing but the expression of the abiding significance of any man in the face of death.

Hence, we cannot be satisfied with the mere fact that Jesus existed. That fact must be elaborated into a statement on who he was and what he said and did. It is clear that we cannot construct a biography of Jesus, yet this need not mean that we know nothing of him, nor that the preaching of the Church is a falsification of his own preaching. Speaking as a systematic theologian, Rahner says that the dogmatic reflection on Faith cannot avoid the conviction that in the actual Jesus there was a sufficient awareness and expression of his function and person to provide a basis for that which Christian dogma confesses of Jesus in its Christology. This knowledge and expression, indeed, came to its fulfillment and legitimation in the Resurrection, which became the vantage point from which the community came to see the real truth about Jesus. Naturally, the self-awareness of Jesus need not be seen as a "verbal identity" with later Christology; but that there be some positive relation is essential to the Christian faith. Even Easter itself could not explain the relation between Jesus and Christology if it did not involve the legitimation of some claim at least implicitly involved in the work of Jesus.

The present state of exegesis has made it clear that Jesus appeared in history as the decisive preacher of the kingdom of God's love so that the realization of that kingdom is intimately associated with his ministry. The basic issue of New Testament Christology is the question as to whether this datum, viewed in retrospect, might be seen as at least implicitly a decisive saving-claim. And if the person of the Messiah be seen as the figure through whom God's kingdom is to be inaugurated, then it would be understandable how it came about that the community should come to see him as Messiah, even though there is no clear and incontestable evidence that he ever used the title of himself. Thus one could see at least the possibility that his disciples had come to hope that he was Messiah already during his ministry. But this hope would have been radically questioned by his violent death. It would be from the perspective of the Easter-experience that they would have come to affirm the vindication of Jesus' mission by God, and thus to see that what they had hoped to be the case was in fact the deepest truth about Jesus. He is in fact the Christ; in his person the rule of God's love has been decisively realized.

In this way significant light is shed on the intimate relation between Jesus and Christ in the New Testament. What first appears as a title eventually becomes a proper name to such an extent that it is interchangeable with the name of Jesus. As Ratzinger writes, the issue of the Christology of the New Testament finally is the affirmation of the unity of his person and work. Jesus is his work; he does not give us a word that is separable from his person. His person is the Word; his person is his teaching, and his teaching is he himself (Ratzinger, p. 148).

A more careful assessment of the New Testament sources, therefore, indicates that the so-called radical cleavage between Jesus and Christology does not really exist in the New Testament. Rather, it is created by certain theologians on the basis of a prior assumption. The early Christological confessions intend to express the "truth about Jesus." This much can be shown historically. Whether, in fact, one accepts that truth always has been and remains an issue of faith.

The viewpoint we have just presented implies that the issue of dogma in a broad sense begins already in the New Testament. We have attempted to show that there is an intrinsic relation between the person of Jesus and the interpretation of the community. There still remains the question of the relation between the New Testament and the dogmatic formulae of the early Church. We cannot give a treatment of the complex history which led this way. Suffice it to say that the New Testament Christology tends to be largely functional, speaking of God and of God's Christ in relation to man and his history. The conciliar dogma, in contrast, is cast in ontological terms.

That such a development should have taken place is understandable if we take into account the tendency of the human mind to ask questions. As soon as one begins to think, one can hardly avoid asking what are the realities about which Scripture speaks in functional and relational terms. Scripture had focused on the radical unity of the person and work of Jesus. Ratzinger argues that, in a different time and place, the dogmas of Nicea and Chalcedon intend to express precisely this radical identity of service and being, of work and of person (Ratzinger, p. 169). Far from being a corruption of the Biblical faith, it is a safeguard that keeps us from reducing Christ to what could have been expected simply in terms of human hopes. If, as Scripture says, he functions as Son of God and as Word, this can be only because, as Nicea and Chalcedon say, he is God; he is God's Word. If as Scripture says, he acted genuinely as man, this can be only because he truly is man. We cannot have Jesus without Christ, nor Christ without Jesus. We are constantly pushed from one to the other since Jesus subsists only as the Christ, and the Christ subsists only in the shape of Jesus.

A study of the history of Christology indicates that the Christological dogma is twofold. It is a statement about the reality of Jesus himself; and it is a statement about the intrinsic relation of Jesus to the salvation of mankind. The dogma is objective in that it intends to speak of the reality of Jesus; it is existential in that it intends to speak of the meaning of Jesus for mankind. Such an understanding of dogma must be distinguished from all attempts to establish some particular psychological datum in the life of Jesus as the basis of Christology, and from all attempts to make Christology totally a function of the community, or — as it appears so often today — a function of isolated individuals. Such attempts have been in the past and remain today the projections of subjective tastes which may or may not have anything to do with Jesus.

Thus, when reduced to its ultimate meaning, some form of Christological dogma seems to be historically inevitable. What the dogma finally means is that what is said about Christ must in some way be grounded in his own personal mystery. But, on the other hand, what is said about

Christ must be, in some way an answer to a question in man; it must correspond to something experienced in our own heart. What Christ is, he is for us; but what he is for us is his own personal mystery. Reflecting the twofold structure of the dogma, the development of Christology must attempt to unfold the meaning of Christ for human life in each new generation; but it must also show how that meaning is grounded in Christ so that Christology is not merely a projection of human aspirations, but truly gives expression to a meeting with God in Christ.

Chapter II
THE PERSON AND THE IMAGE

It has been characteristic of Christianity from its very inception that it appeals for its primary insights not to some sort of cosmic-mystical experience nor to a metaphysical doctrine, but first and foremost to an historical personage, Jesus of Nazareth, in whom the Christian believes one is to find the basic clue as to the nature of God and of man. If it is to be true to itself, therefore, Christian faith must remain always in contact with that historical foundation; and from that base, it develops its proper understanding of God and of man, and of God's way of dealing with man in history.

If we were to try to retrace the steps of the

Church's journey to its Christological confession, our route would have to follow the experience of the Lord's early followers who, as is clear from Scripture, experienced Jesus first of all and obviously as a man. Not only were they uncertain as to the precise meaning of Jesus and his ministry, but at times they were obviously mistaken. Their way begins not with a blazing theophany, but with the experience of a man from a poverty-ridden family from a back-water town in Galilee. How difficult it must have been for them to move from that experience to the confession that "Jesus is Lord" becomes clear from a careful reading of the New Testament.

We have so accustomed ourselves to say that Jesus was true God that we tend to lose a feeling for the peculiar quality of the Christian confession. Christian faith begins not with a clear experience of what God is which it then relates to Jesus. Rather, quite the reverse, it begins with the experience of a human being who finally is seen to break out of the limits of human concepts and expectations. From that experience eventually the Old Testament concept of God had to be expanded. And in as far as that human life is seen as the embodiment of the very Word of God and receives the divine seal in the Resurrection, it appears as the paradigm of the genuine, full human possibility. Jesus appears — in Paul's words — as the Second Man; as the embodiment of what God intends man to be from the dawn of creation (1 Cor 15: 45–49).

Recent historical and exegetical studies have

led to a critical assessment of the standard handbook image of Christ. This image, we must point out, is not to be identified with the Christological dogma of the councils. Rather, it is an image which emerges from a particular style of theological speculation in which the dogma is interpreted on the basis of certain philosophical principles. Characteristic of this style is the fact that it says not only is Jesus fully human, but that he is perfectly human; and the meaning of that perfection is read from the Aristotelian view which identifies perfection with knowledge. Thus emerges the image of Jesus as one who, in his human mind, possessed relative omniscience from the first moment of his existence.

Practically every systematic Christology in Roman Catholic circles deals with Jesus' humanity in these terms, and official documents of popes and of the Holy Office reinforce the image to such an extent that it has assumed normative significance in the minds of many Catholics. If one were to pin-point the full implication of this image in a few words, one could say that Jesus appears as one who has no genuine human history. Indeed, he has a biological history, but there can be no talk of a development of knowledge and of self-awareness. It is important to recognize that this image is not dogma in the strict sense. It is an image that can legitimately be called into question; and, in fact, recent attempts to respect the findings of exegesis have led to new assessments of the integral humanity of Jesus.

This venture is not a mere substitution of superficial images that emerge from arbitrary, personal preferences. On the contrary, we are here concerned with a basic change in methodology which is of far-reaching significance. At its most profound level, it is a shift from a non-historical methodology to one that is self-consciously historical. We are, therefore, looking at Jesus and at the history of the community's interpretations of Jesus in as far as possible through the methodology of historical-critical research. In this sense, some basic knowledge of the sort of person Jesus was becomes very important indeed. And yet, the history of exegetical studies has made it sufficiently clear that we are not in a position to write a biography of Jesus since the sources do not provide information of the sort that would be required for such a project. As often as one attempts to create such a biography, the results tell more about the subjective preferences of the author than they tell about Jesus. Neither are we suggesting that Christology is to be reduced to a search for an ethical model. This has never been the direct point of the Church's kerygma nor of the later dogma, though at some level it must enter into Christology.

What we are concerned with primarily is what we may know historically about that which in faith is confessed to be an Incarnation of God's Word. Any attempt to make sense out of the history of the New Testament and of later Christology must be willing to distinguish between historical facts in a positive sense and theological facts in the sense of faith-inspired interpretations of the facts. It is with these two dimensions that a healthy Christology operates. At the first level, there was a man named Jesus of Nazareth about whose life and career we do not have a great amount of information; but we do have sufficient knowledge to make some important judgments to which we will refer later. He was born of an impoverished family and confined his activity to a small nation. He left no works of literature or art to enrich the human community. He lived a life of poverty as he preached the coming of the kingdom of God, suffering a violent death by execution at the hands of the Romans. His was not a glorious existence; it in no way conforms to spectacular expectations. In fact, it seems a fairly ordinary existence of a man who appeared to some of his contemporaries as a noble preacher. And yet, it is of this sort of life that Christians have come to say that it is the Incarnation of the very Word of God.

Whitehead phrased it well when he wrote: "The essence of Christianity is the appeal to the life of Christ as a revelation of the nature of God and of His agency in the world. The record is fragmentary, inconsistent, and uncertain. It is not necessary for me to express any opinion as to the proper reconstruction of the most likely tale of historic fact . . . But there can be no doubt as to what elements in the record have evoked a response from all that is best in human nature. The Mother, the Child, the bare manger: the lowly man, homeless and self-forgetful, with his message of peace, love, and sympathy: the suffering, the agony, the tender words as life ebbed, the final despair; and the whole with the authority of supreme victory . . . Can there be any doubt that the power of Christianity lies in its revelation in act of that which Plato divined in theory?" (*Adventures of Ideas,* [Toronto, 1965] p. 167). To have recovered some sense of these beginnings is to be overpowered by the bold audacity of the Christian faith.

When we speak of Jesus, we are using the proper name of a man about whom we can say a number of things of an historical nature. When, on the other hand, we speak of Christ, we are using not a name but a title that expresses the faith of the early community. It is at first one among many titles; but eventually the title, Christ, came to be the most characteristic title and from it the very name of the community is derived. This distinction is important, for it brings into sharp focus the kinds of questions involved in the historical understanding of Christianity. We are dealing always with the history of a man and with the history of the community's faith-interpretation of him.

From the start there have been these two poles: Jesus himself; and that which others have thought of him. "Who do people say I am?" (Mk 8: 27). Many answers might be given to that question, and Mark lists several that were current at this time: John the Baptist, Elijah, or one of the prophets. To these we might add answers offered more recently: an itinerant Jewish rabbi, a great ethical teacher, a religious fanatic, a mythological projection of man's desire to be divine. These may contain some element of truth, but in general, they miss the mark because they see Jesus simply as one human being among many; extra-ordinary, important, interesting, but not truly unique. They are all answers that fail to see Jesus as the living embodiment of God's love for men.

But, Mark tells us, Jesus put another question to his disciples: "But you, who do you say I am?" (Mk 8: 29). Here he is asking those who are committed to him in a personal way to state their convictions about him. Peter spoke up and said: "You are the Christ" (Mk 8: 29). Peter's answer, as is clear in the Gospels, can be given only on the basis of faith. But it is also clear that Peter's answer is given in terms of a Jewish religious culture. Christians of every age are called upon to give an answer to that question. Since it is the same Jesus we are speaking of, there must be something the same in our response; but since our culture, history and world-view are different, there should also be a difference. It is of basic importance for believers to express what Jesus means for them; but it is equally important to show how their Christology relates to Jesus himself, and hence to test their interpretations against the interpretation(s) of Scripture and the tradition of the Church. For if we are not willing to do that, then our Christ-image may be only the expression of what we think is important; it may have nothing to do with Jesus himself.

When Christology is approached historically, a number of important qualities emerge: Christology takes place in community; it takes place in a history; and it has always been multiple. First, it takes place in a community. So it has been from the early days of the New Testament community. Faith in Jesus involves a community of believers; it is never merely the private possession of individuals. And each individual must be willing to test his Christ-image against those of others. But this community itself has a history as does the interpretation it has placed on Jesus. No one standing in the second half of the twentieth century can determine what Jesus should mean without the faith that began in New Testament times and has been passed on through the centuries. The only concrete link between him and us is the faith-community in which his memory is preserved. Only within that world of faith can one perceive Jesus as the Christ, and only by referring our Christ-image back to Jesus himself can we be freed of the limits of our own subjectivity.

The communal and historical dimensions lead unavoidably to the third quality. Already in the New Testament we find many titles referred to Jesus. No one of them is adequate; each expresses something different from the others. But what they have in common is the fact that they see in him a real human being who is the embodiment and the presence of God's love and forgiveness and mercy for man.

Later Church history also shows that Christology is multiple. There have always been a plurality of Christologies, and there are many today. But each of these must deal with the same elements that are basic to Scripture: 1) the firm conviction that in some way we meet God in Jesus; 2) that the Jesus in whom we meet God is a genuine, historically conditioned human being; 3) that the God whom we meet in this man and the man in whom we meet God are related in a way that is not accidental, but in a relationship so intimate that it is best conceived after the analogy of personal union (N. Pittenger, *Christology Reconsidered* [SCM Press, 1970] p. 7).

It takes only a little reflection to see how these elements are reflected in the Creed. They are the constantly voiced convictions of the Christian community about Jesus of Nazareth: that he is true man; that he is true God; that Jesus is personally one with God. These are the elements which must enter into any Christology that would lay claim to even minimal adequacy. Yet there have always been tensions in the efforts of Christians to hold these together in an intelligible unity. There have been, from the earliest centuries, denials of his divinity. Of this we might say that those believe too little who see him merely as one of several great historical figures; an example and pattern for all; a man whose ethical teaching we applaud and try to follow, but who is finally, not significantly different from other men.

There have been those also, from the earliest years, who have denied his full humanity. This has taken various forms. Against this St. John could write: "We proclaim to you what we have seen and touched and heard with our ears; we saw it and testify to it" (1 Jn 1: 1–4). Those believe too much who see him only as a divine being, as God dressed up as a man, as one who from the moment of his birth knew all things and was in complete and perfect control of himself and his environment, as if he were not human in any form recognizable to us. Yet, if we are to be true to Scripture and to the Creed, we must recognize in Jesus a full, genuine humanity, neither more nor less than ours. If that which God has done for the world in Jesus is not done in one who is fully human, then of what significance can it be for the rest of us who are human beings?

Chapter III
THE STORY OF JESUS

Christology always involves a looking back at Jesus' life from the perspective of Easter. For those who are willing to take the critical studies of exegesis seriously it is clear that we cannot have the type of clarity about the life of Jesus that we sometimes imagine. Yet we can ask what the life of Jesus looked like; what sort of man he appeared to be to his disciples; and what relation there is between his life-work and the Easter proclamation of the early community; for the preaching of the Church has never been a simple continuation of the preaching of Jesus. In the final analysis, Christian faith in the proper sense emerges from both sides of the Easter-experience; i.e. from the life and activity of Jesus and from the experience and preaching of the post-Easter community. While it is not possible to write anything approaching a biography of Jesus, yet it is possible to know that which appears as fundamental in a critical understanding of the relation of Faith to the history of Jesus.

While there is remarkable diversity among exegetes about the interpretation of certain facts, yet there is an area of consensus among scholars of varied backgrounds. It is with this area of consensus that we are concerned; and in the light of it we can responsibly assume a viewpoint that lies between a radical historical skepticism on the one hand and a naive fundamentalism on the other. The material involved here is important in that it points to the heart of Jesus' mission and the meaning of his life. Following the lead of exegetes, we divide our reflections into three sections: 1) his preaching, 2) his actions, 3) his execution.

The clearest thing we know about Jesus is that his entire public life was dominated by the proclamation of God's rule, or the kingdom of God. Matthew describes his ministry in the following way: "And He went about all Galilee, teaching in their synagogues and preaching the gospel of the kingdom, and healing every disease and every infirmity among the people" (Mt 4: 23). And Mark writes: ". . . Jesus came into Galilee, preaching the gospel of the kingdom of God, and saying, 'The time is fulfilled, and the kingdom of God is at hand. Repent and believe in the gospel.'" (Mk 1: 14,15). And Luke says: "The kingdom of God is not coming with signs to be observed; nor will they say, 'Lo, here it is!' for behold, the kingdom of God is in the midst of you" (Lk 17: 20,21). We must ask, then, what is meant by the rule or the kingdom of God.

This term comes from the Old Testament and refers to the Jewish expectation that the promises of God to Israel would be fulfilled. As a part of the Old Testament, the term itself has a history. Israel's faith already in the Abraham-tradition was a faith that looked to a future fulfillment. In the case of Abraham, it would be the Land of Promise and numerous descendants. Earthy as this expectation was, yet it would be a gift of God who would be faithful to his promises. Israel always looked forward to such a fulfillment, and late in the Old Testament a wide range of ideas developed concerning it. Some expected it to take the form of the restoration of Jewish national unity; others expected it to be a universal state of harmony and peace; some expected it to be within history; others thought it would lie beyond history. Diverse as these ideas may be, they have in common the idea that God would intervene in human experience and would establish among men a final and decisive state of harmony, peace, and reconciliation. The kingdom of God, then, involves a decisive turning-point in man's history; a point at which God would bring man's life to that fullness and completion which God intended for it from the beginning. What this meant for most of Jesus' contemporaries was a political kingdom full of material blessings.

It was in such a context that Jesus grew up and undertook his mission of proclaiming the gospel of the kingdom. But we can notice a number of far-reaching differences. Jesus took up the expectation of his people, but transformed it in a radical way, freeing it of political-nationalistic elements and giving it a universal meaning. The rule of God is not to be thought of as the power of an oriental potentate who dominates over his subjects. Rather, it is the rule of a Father's tender love expressed in so many ways in the parables of the merciful Father, the Prodigal Son, the Lost Sheep, and others. The kingdom of God will not be a political force, as becomes clear from the Temptation accounts; rather it will be that condition where men allow the call of God's love to be the guiding norm and spirit of their lives. If God reaches freely and unreservedly to us in love, can we be satisfied with less as our response to him. Thus, in Jesus' teaching the coming of the kingdom is always associated with conversion or repentance. There must be an interior change in man; he must move from a self-centered life to a God-centered life. The kingdom in Jesus' preaching does not mean a liberation from the political yoke of Rome, but shaking off the restrictions of our own egoism with all its limitations, and allowing the demands of God's love to work themselves out in our lives.

Jesus shared the hopes of his people for the rule of God, but he understood this not to involve a divine intervention in power or force. Rather, he saw it as the call of God to a new way of life through which the sick relations of man to his fellow-man would be healed and man would find the wholeness he so keenly desires.

Of importance also in Jesus' preaching is the fact that the coming of the kingdom is most intimately associated with his own person. For Jesus, the kingdom is not something that lies far off in the future. Rather, God is establishing his rule in the very person and work of Jesus. Hence, the sense of presence and of urgency in his preaching: "for behold, the kingdom of God is in the midst of you" (Lk 17: 21). Jesus not only proclaims the kingdom; He brings it. "But if it is through the finger of God that I cast out devils, then know that the kingdom of God has overtaken you" (Lk 11: 20).

Even more, Jesus is the kingdom in his own person; he is God's rule in person. Hence Matthew writes: "Blessed are the eyes that have seen what you have seen" (Mt 13: 6). As exegetes point out, the figure of Jesus really fits into none of the religious or political categories of his time. At times he is called rabbi, but he does not merely explain Torah as a rabbi would. He appears as a new Moses with a new and decisive word of God. At times he is called prophet, but he does not use the typical prophetic formula "thus says the Lord." On the contrary, his typical formula is, "Amen, I say to you." As exegete

Ernst Käsemann says, it is as though he is God's own mouth rather than a mere mouth-piece.

The present state of exegesis would warrant the conclusion that Jesus appeared in history as the decisive witness to the rule of God's Fatherly love that is breaking into history in Jesus' person and ministry. His life is one of faithfulness to the demands of the Father's love. His call to repentance is a call to live a life of trust in the Father's loving power and to allow the demands of love to penetrate all dimensions of our life; for only then will God rule among men.

The meaning of Jesus' preaching becomes even more clear when it is viewed in relation to his actions. Exegetes have pointed out that the tradition about the actions of Jesus are clustered around the core of his preaching and stand in the Old Testament tradition of prophetic acts, a prophetic act being the symbolic acting-out of something that is about to take place.

The tradition concerning the actions of Jesus in relation to sinners and outcasts is one of the most certain facts of the tradition about Jesus. In the quotation from Matthew given at the beginning of this chapter, we notice the immediate connection between the preaching of Jesus and the signs in behalf of the sick and the weak. Throughout the Gospels, we notice Jesus' constant association with sinners and outcasts of all sorts. And most pointedly, we notice his table-fellowship with sinners, much to the scandal of those who represented the official Jewish religion. In the context of Judaism, to share a meal with another was something sacred. Indeed, the meal had become another symbol for the kingdom of God, presenting this as a state where men would sit down together to share in the life, mercy, and forgiveness of God. Thus, when Jesus sits down to table with the outcasts and the rejected, he is acting out the banquet of the kingdom. Such an action on the part of Jesus has little to do with social criticism, reform, or political revolution. His behavior is to be understood in relation to his preaching of the presence of the kingdom.

Such an action involves a reversal of those standards that see wealth and power as signs of God's favor. It also tells us that it is not those who "justify" themselves by fulfilling legal prescriptions that will be saved. The condition for entrance into the kingdom is that we recognize our need for the physician. Thus, Jesus' behavior toward the sick and the sinners is an acting out of the call to conversion; and sitting at table with such people is an acting out of the kingdom as a sharing in the life, mercy, and forgiveness of God for those who are open to receive it. Communion with Jesus means communion with God. Jesus acts out God's relation to man.

Gradually it becomes more clear that man's relation to God is associated with his relation to Jesus. Ever more clearly he appears as the decisive witness to God's kingdom so that the destiny of other men is tied up with their relation to Jesus himself. This becomes even more pointed in those texts that present the call to discipleship, for the bond of the disciple with Jesus goes far beyond anything that would be expected of an ordinary rabbi. Anyone who would follow him must risk all. He who hears the call and rejects it will be rejected by God (Lk 12: 8,9).

If we today ask the early followers of Jesus what sort of man he was, the answer we receive is that he impressed them as the decisive witness to God's kingdom of love, as one who called them to decide for or against God. Indeed, their own relation to God was essentially intertwined with their relation to Jesus. If we ask further to what did Jesus call them, the answer would be "to live a life of trust in the Father's love." To build a life on any other foundation is to build on sand because every created thing and every created person can betray us. It is only the Father's love that we can trust with absolute seriousness. If we build a life on that foundation, we will be freed from undue and restricting dependence on anything else.

It is clear that Jesus came into conflict with the influential groups of his time. As Vawter phrases it, he was executed as a consequence of carrying out his mission as he saw it (Vawter, p. 68). The meaning of both his teaching and his actions is focused in the cross. What is one to say about the fact that the preacher of the kingdom of God's love meets such a violent death? Certainly it must have made the disciples wonder. What kind of love is it that allows its witness to be destroyed? How is it possible to trust in such a power? Or does that power exist at all? In this sense, the whole burden of Jesus' mission is raised on the cross; for his death calls into question the truth of what he had preached. If his story ends finally with his death, he would hardly become a source of hope for us; for then he would appear to be an innocent murder-victim, and his life would be a basis for skepticism rather than for hope. Hence, we can see that without the proclamation of the Resurrection, faith in Jesus would be without a basis and without a point.

It is the Easter-experience of the Risen Lord that lifts the veil from the eyes of the disciples so that they can say: Despite the fact that he was rejected by almost all of his contemporaries, and that he was doubted even by themselves, his closest friends, yet he was right. The Father has accepted him and his witness; he lives with the Father and the mystery of God's love has come to its full realization in him. Now they can say truly he is the Christ, the Son of the Living God.

From that point onward, it becomes possible for all who believe in Jesus to see their own lives in a new way. All experience misunderstanding and betrayal; most wonder at times whether there is any point to life at all. But he shows us a model of courage and faithfulness in trying to do God's will; and that will calls us always to a life of love and concern. He shows that God does not measure the worth of a person by external success, but that his love calls to everyone and requires the willingness to say we need God to carry out our lives well. To live for the kingdom means to try, within our own limits, to do what we can to bring love to heal the sickness of human life; and to do this without regard for social status. He has shown us that God is always ready to forgive us. And when the burden of life weighs most heavily on our shoulders and we are tempted to think it is all pointless in the final analysis, he assures us that such a life is accepted by God; that every man who sincerely tries to live this way, faithful to the requirements of God's love, will find a deeper, richer, fuller life with God in the kingdom of the Father.

Chapter IV
PUT TO DEATH FOR OUR SINS

As we indicated earlier, Christology must be willing to deal with certain common historical facts as well as with the interpretation of these facts in a faith-context. This is true not only of the life of Jesus, but of his death as well; that death which Christians proclaim as a sacrifice for the forgiveness of sin.

The historical facts concerning the death of Jesus seem ordinary enough. As Vawter indicates, his death would appear as a rather commonplace execution, both politically and religiously motivated, in which both Romans and Jews were implicated (Vawter, p. 56ff.). Details concerning his arrest and trial are varied and inconsistent;

and it is difficult to determine the precise nature of the role played by the Roman and Jewish leaders. This question is complicated by the fact that, as we have already seen, the person of Jesus fits into none of the current roles, whether political or religious, while on the other hand, it is possible to associate him with many contemporary nationalist movements. Yet it would be true to say that Jesus was executed as a direct consequence of fulfilling his mission as he saw it.

Had he foreseen it himself? Had he predicted it to his disciples? In general, the predictions as they now stand in the New Testament may well be constructions of the early community. On the other hand, it may well be that Jesus did, at least toward the end of his ministry, foresee that if things continued in the way they were going, a deadly conflict with the vested interests of religious and political powers was inevitable. In this sense, we may be dealing with something like a prophetic insight rather than with clear, detailed knowledge. If he had given precise information about his imminent death, it would be difficult to account for the confusion and despair of the disciples.

Concerning the historical facts of his death, then, we may conclude that to an historian, it would appear as a rather ordinary execution that was politically and religiously motivated, and may well have been foreseen by Jesus as the consequence of fulfilling his mission (Vawter, p. 68). If his mission may be said to involve a saving-claim, the death which came as a consequence thereof may well have been seen by Jesus as having a saving-significance. If we may justifiably speak of a "hidden Christology" implicit in Jesus' ministry, we may also speak of a "hidden soteriology" in reference to his understanding of his death (Kasper, p. 141).

We have so accustomed ourselves to speak of the death of Jesus as a sacrifice for sin that we lose sight of the fact that it was first of all a serious problem for the disciples. Their attempts to understand it and to interpret it have led to various models both in Scripture and in later tradition. Surely, prior to their Easter-experience, the violence of his death must have destroyed or at least severely shaken their hopes in him. And even after Easter, in the conviction that despite his death, he had been vindicated by God, it is not at all clear why his path should have led to the violence of the cross. If he was, indeed, the decisive prophet of the kingdom of God's love, could not the loving power of God have seen fit to acknowledge him earlier? Could not a God of love have removed the ambiguity of his life and have made his meaning clear without that death?

It is important to keep in mind that the first Christian confession is the proclamation of the Resurrection. From that starting-point, the eyes of the first disciples would have looked to the future, to the soon-to-be-expected return of the Lord. But as time went on, their attention would have begun to look back to his life and death.

The New Testament indicates a search for acceptable patterns to give expression to a belief that underlies the variety of patterns, and which may be said to be independent of the patterns, or at least of any particular pattern. As Vawter writes, the basic conviction from which the early Christians proceeded was the conviction that the new life of the Spirit which they experienced was due entirely to what God had done in the crucified and resurrected Christ. Faith in the risen Lord is faith in one whose life and death had somehow served God's purpose in bringing about the salvific event of the resurrection (Vawter, p. 80). Any attempt to speak of the saving character of his death cannot isolate it from his Resurrection, on the one side, and from his life, on the other side.

Early efforts to give expression to the meaning of his death are varied. The Gospel of Mark, making use of Old Testament traditions, presents Jesus' death as a result of the rejection of God's love by a blind and sinful world. To Matthew, the death of Jesus appears as an apocalyptic event bringing with it the end of the old age and the beginning of the new. Somewhat different is the emphasis of Luke for whom the cross is seen as the place of forgiveness. In John, yet another perspective appears; for here the death of Jesus is the hour of his glorification, the moment of the giving of the Spirit as he gives his spirit over to the Father. John, who consistently brings glory and earthly existence together throughout his Gospel, now brings glory and crucifixion into

42

such close proximity that the Jesus raised on the cross is raised into his hour of glory. The dying Jesus is the risen Lord, who is returning to the Father in the hour of death. Good Friday, Easter, Ascension, Pentecost virtually coincide. The crucified one is the exalted one, and the hour of the crucifixion is the birth of the Church. The crucified Jesus is the new Paschal Lamb from whose side flow the sacraments of baptism and Eucharist.

The death of Jesus is but one event at a particular time and place in history, yet each of the Gospels expresses different dimensions of its meaning. It is an event that no theology has expressed in its completeness. As Paul writes, in the face of the cross of Christ, our wisdom appears as foolishness (1 Cor 1: 20). Not only do we find the death of Jesus presented from a plurality of perspectives, but we find a plurality of symbolic models as well. From among the various models found in the New Testament, it was the sacrifice model, developed so extensively in *Hebrews,* that has come to have such a pervasive hold on Christian consciousness.

The ease with which Christians speak of Jesus' death as a sacrifice often obscures the deeper meaning of this model. Frequently it is conceived on the analogy of ritual sacrifices in which men offered animals and gifts of the earth to placate angry gods. One attempts to surmount the human feeling of guilt by conciliatory gestures. With that framework in mind, one begins to think of the death of Jesus as an act of conciliation offered to an angry God whose rigid sense of justice refuses to be placated by anything less than a human sacrifice in the most painful and horrendous conditions.

This sort of transfer from the extra-biblical religions to the mystery of Christ is untrue both to the prophetic tradition of the Old Testament and to the whole of the New Testament. How often does the Old Testament tell the Jews that God is weary of all their sacrifices; that what God really desires is the sacrifice of the human heart (Ps 50: 9–14). The New Testament theology of the cross, standing in harmony with this Old Testament tradition, reverses the core reality of sacrifice; for the cross of Christ is not the embodiment of man's attempts to manipulate God. It is not man who goes to God with conciliatory gifts; rather it is God who comes to man. "God is in Christ reconciling the world to himself" (2 Cor 5: 19). As Ratzinger has argued, "With this twist in the idea of expiation, and thus in the whole axis of religion, worship too, man's whole existence, acquires in Christianity a new direction. Worship follows in Christianity first of all in thankful acceptance of the divine deed of salvation" (Ratzinger, p. 214-215).

A fuller reading of the New Testament indicates that while the redemptive work is first of all God's act in and for man, and therefore represents a descending line; at the same time, the New Testament reflects an ascending line in the pure obedience of Jesus. That which the presence of God evokes in Jesus is the perfect, human acceptance of and pursuit of the Father's will. Thus, the New Testament reflects a dialogical understanding of religion which is fundamentally personalist in tone.

In the *Epistle to the Hebrews,* the entire process of Jesus' death and glorification is described in reference to the Old Testament Day of Atonement. Jesus ascends the cross as both priest and victim in what may be seen as his earthly liturgy. His sacrifice is begun on earth and brought to completion in heaven where he carries out his heavenly liturgy as eternal priest in the presence of the Father. The theological assessment of this theology must be made in the clear awareness that Jesus was not a priest but a layman by Old Testament standards; and what is referred to as the sacrifice of atonement is not a rite carried out in a temple or church, but the real suffering and death of a real man.

The implication of *Hebrews* would seem to be that the reality of atonement, expiation, and union with God is not accomplished through ritual activity, however elaborate and extensive it may be. Such activity, as it is here reflected in the Day of Atonement, expresses the deep desire of man to find forgiveness and union with God; so the ritual activity of man arises from a profound human concern. But in the final analysis, it is the symbolic expression of a relation between man and God that is realized in the living reality of Jesus. And if we probe into the depths of that mystery, what we discover is a life that is one of pure disposability to the will of God for the sake of mankind. This sort of life, which is a response to the prior presence of God, and which is brought to its fullness in the acceptance of that life by the Father, is the only true cult. It is, according to *Hebrews,* the cult on which the salvation of the world depends. The deepest meaning of Jesus' cult is his *Yes* to the will of His Father; a *Yes* that is carried out concretely in his existence as Servant-Son and finds its final historical expression in the body that is broken and the blood that is poured out.

Echoing this theology several centuries later, Augustine sees Christ as the one who became sacrifice totally. Sacrifice is not something other than himself. It is finally his very life of love for God and man, which culminates in his death in such a way that his arms outstretched on the cross appear as a symbol of his twofold love; a love that is open to the Father's will as it extends itself in mercy to mankind.

For centuries Christians have spoken of the sacrificial death of Jesus in terms of the satisfaction theory. What most are less familiar with is the fact that this is a time-conditioned mode of expressing a theological concern, and that it is not the only model possible. As a theory, it is felt to be inadequate in a number of significant ways. Drawing some of its basic concepts from the realm of Roman law and Germanic notions of justice, it tends to present the meaning of the death of Jesus in strongly ethical terms, overlooking the long-standing tradition of cosmic theories of redemption so characteristic of the

East and found as well in certain theologians of the West. Concentrating on sin as an infinite offense, and conceiving the relation between man and God as analogous to earthly legal orders, this view sees the need for an infinite satisfaction to restore the order of justice. Thus it concludes to the necessity of an incarnation of a divine person, for man cannot offer that infinite satisfaction. Another weakness of the theory lies in the fact that it fails to show any inner connection between the death of Jesus and the redemption effected by that death. In most popular versions, we hear that — given the Incarnation — any act of Jesus would have been adequate for effecting man's salvation. While in fact we are redeemed by the blood of the Crucified, actually — had God so chosen — mankind could have been redeemed by any act of obedience at any time of Jesus' life. Thus, any real significance for Jesus' personal history is effectively ruled out.

The theory of satisfaction has its finger on a key theological issue when it locates the primary significance of the death of Jesus precisely in the fact that it is an act of loving obedience which found expression in the passion and the Crucifixion. Its greatest weakness rests in the fact that it does not and cannot show why it is precisely in the death of Jesus — and not in just any ethical act of his life — that salvation is effected.

Contemporary theologians have called attention to both the truth and to the limits of the dominant Western model for interpreting the meaning of Jesus' death. Theologians such as Rahner have attempted to show that it was precisely a death that was required for the realization of salvation, and that such salvation could not have been effected by any other ethical act of Jesus. In speaking this way, we must keep in mind that salvation is not to be thought of merely in negative terms as the forgiveness of sin, but also in positive terms as the fulfillment of created reality in the immediate presence of the incomprehensible mystery of God.

What is needed, Rahner argues, is a more adequate philosophical understanding of the meaning of death and its relation to human life. (*On the Theology of Death, passim.*) While all multicellular forms of life die in the sense that their organization as living beings disintegrates — and man shares this fate with all material, living beings — yet the reality of death for man is more than biological disintegration. In fact, for man death is a human phenomenon the meaning of which is related to the character of human life. Man exists, so writes Rahner, as one for whom the fact and meaning of existence is a mystery. Man is a questioning being, capable of asking the what and the why of everything that comes his way, including himself and his own existence. Man is a questioner who goes through life hoping and trying to create a meaningful existence. Yet when faced with death, he is faced with the question as to whether his existence with all the "little meanings" he has tried to create is finally of any real significance at all. The moment of death, therefore, appears as a peculiar human moment, involving not only the breakdown of the organism as something imposed on man by as yet uncontrollable biological laws, but a peculiarly human way of relating to this fact. Thus, as Rahner sees it, death is not only something suffered by man, but something actively engaged in by man as a free being disposing of himself in the face of an incomprehensible and incalculable mystery. Death is, in this view, the final moment of a personal history that has been prepared for by the whole of the life that has preceded it. It is an attack from without in which man experiences utterly the extent of his limitations; but it is simultaneously an active perfecting of oneself from within.

The moment of death is the end of a personal history in which man seeks meaning in his life. Since it is the final moment of a history, it shares all the darkness and ambiguity of that history. And if all of man's historical relations to the world are tainted by sin, then his death also will be affected by the reality of sin. Rahner concludes that if salvation is to be understood as the fulfillment of man as a personal center of knowledge and love, whether he had sinned or not, it would require as a necessary condition a history of free self-determination which would find its most fully human moment in the act of dying. And if, further, man's situation is that of a sinner, then the experience of dying will be the more obscure and painful.

From such reflections, Rahner concludes that any fulfillment of man's history would involve a death. But even more to the point, any salvation from our sinful situation by an Incarnation of the Word of God would be a salvation in and through death. The death of Jesus is not simply the result of an arbitrary decree on the part of the Father who could have been satisfied with any other act of Jesus as satisfaction. In singling out the death of Jesus in this way, we must keep in mind that his death must be seen in relation to his entire personal history. Without that history, such a death would have been impossible. But without death, the history would have been an incomplete and unfulfilled existence; for history is, by definition, the unfinished movement of man toward final perfection. Life and death stand in an inseparable unity.

In brief, Rahner argues that an Incarnation into a sinful condition, and any salvation from a sinful situation can ultimately take place only when man stands as an utterly free agent before the Mystery encountered at the limits of life and experiences the depths of creaturehood and finitude; and precisely in that moment accepts the mystery of being absolutely disposed of, thus placing the final stamp on his life. Only death in the darkness of a sinful situation could terminate a real Incarnation into the sinful condition of man.

The death of Jesus, then, is unavoidably related to the style of his human life; it is the final *Yes* to the mysterious will of the Father, the pursuit of which has lead Jesus to such dire straits. It presupposes the entire history of his faithful obedience, and is in fact the final perfection of that obedience.

If sin is a disordered turning to self and the world, then the overcoming of sin will be effected only by the proper turning to God in a way that calls into question all human idols up to and including the last of all idols: the self. Jesus' life was one in which all man-made idols were called into question. It was a life of pure disposability to the will of the Father for the sake of man. It is pure exodus; going out of self to the Other. It is the perfect counterpart to sin — the standing in oneself.

The death of Jesus, therefore, embodies the most basic Christian understanding of the nature of man. Man's being is to be thoroughly a going-out; a disposability to the Other. Jesus dies as a victim of love to show: 1) that the fuller life of man in history is possible only on the condition that he die the many "little deaths"; 2) that the final power of death is broken; for it need not be seen as a useless destruction, but can become an act of fulfilling praise leading to the fullest possibilities of life in loving communion with God.

The violence of the crucifixion expresses the painful cost of love. Thus, when we look at our own life, we find unavoidably the presence of other people which places limits on us just as surely as it offers greater possibilities. It is very important how we relate to those limits. A cross emerges between our tendency to self-will and the demanding presence of the other. To respond to those limits by rejecting the reality of the other is sin. To respond positively in concern, trust, fidelity, and love is to turn pain into sacrifice; it is to die the "little death." We are dealing not with a cult of suffering, but with a vision of how suffering can be made into a creative, transforming power in human life. Christ did not promise to remove suffering, but he showed how to live with it.

And death itself may be seen not as an encounter with absurdity and annihilation, but as an exodus into the fullest realization of human existence, into loving communion with God. Death, when viewed from the perspective of Christ, is no longer a threat of destruction, but the fulfilling and perfecting act of human life. In this sense, we may say that the power of death is overcome for those who confess the act of God in Jesus Christ.

Chapter V
RAISED FOR OUR JUSTIFICATION

If Jesus is not risen, we are "false witnesses of God; our faith is vain, and we are the most miserable of men" (1 Cor 15: 14–19). What is common to Christians is their confession of the Resurrection. But at the present time, there is a wide spectrum of opinion as to how the Resurrection is to be understood. Again, as we might suspect, the problems begin in the area of exegesis; but a more honest assessment of some of the exegetical positions would indicate that they are not strictly exegetical. Rather, they are theological positions developed by exegetes on the basis of prior assumptions of a philosophical nature.

The proper method for determining the meaning of the New Testament Resurrection texts should not begin by asking the question of relevance. Rather, it should proceed by placing the texts in their proper context and attempting to establish their original intention prior to asking the question of relevance.

In a broad sense, the context of the Resurrection texts can be described as a religious horizon which included a profound confidence in the fidelity of a gracious God. In a more specific sense, it is an eschatological and apocalyptic context in the sense in which these dimensions had been developed in the later prophets and in the period immediately prior to the time of Christ. Jewish eschatology at the time of the New Testament was varied. Some seemed to have little interest in it; some seemed quite nationalistic in their expectations. Sectarian groups such as Qumran and the Essenes developed apocalyptic motifs extensively. Belief in the final resurrection of the dead, where it was accepted, was generally understood quite literally. Such a belief derives its substance from the conviction that God is the source of all life, and it points to the fulfillment of a purpose inherent in creation from the beginning. The resurrection of the dead is seen as an element in the complex reality of the *eschaton* which would represent the consummation of history. Because of this eschatological quality, it is understandable that such resurrection-hopes were generally of a collective character; for they looked to the resurrection of all the redeemed at the end of history. It is within such a context that we must place the ministry of Jesus, and only if we are willing to deal with the Easter-texts in this context can we hope to let them speak for themselves.

When we follow such a procedure, we feel constrained to agree with Schlier that the most obvious intent of these texts is to say that Jesus really lives in his own individual reality with his Father. In other words, the event of Jesus' rising is not merely and entirely an event conjured up in the minds of the disciples; the faith of the disciples relates to the Resurrection as to a mystery which precedes faith. In terms of the context described above, the Easter proclamation is best seen as the proclamation that God's decisive act has been realized in Jesus who died on the cross yet really lives in the kingdom of the Father's loving, life-giving power. The kingdom which Jesus preached as the future of mankind has been realized in him so that his destiny is the anticipation of what God intends for mankind. As the eschatological act of God, the Resurrection is also the vindication of the claim implicit in Jesus' ministry. Hence, in the awareness of the Resurrection, the disciples are able to see the deepest truth about his life. His fidelity was not pointless, nor was he the victim of a delusion. His life did not end in failure, for his lonely death opened into a new and deeper life of perfect communion with the Father. His resurrection is not a mere living on in the hearts and minds of others, nor is it a return to his biological history. It is not the destruction of his humanity, but the fulfillment thereof, for the total love of Jesus that led him ineluctably to the cross is completed in his total going to the Father who accepts all that has been effected in and by that humanity.

How was it that the disciples came to make such a proclamation? To this no definite answer can be given. But in approaching the question, it would be helpful to distinguish between Resurrection and Easter. By Resurrection, we refer to the destiny of Jesus beyond death; to the vindication of his mission by the life-giving act of God in Jesus. By Easter, we refer to the experience of the disciples which gave rise to the conviction that Jesus lives. Christian faith has its origins specifically in the unexpected appearance of the conviction that the one who was crucified is not dead but lives. If we ask, further, what gave rise to this conviction, the answer is found in the experiences described in Scripture as appearances. These appearances must be placed in the broader religious context within which they occurred; and this is a context which, as we have indicated above, includes the hope for life with God for the just; for God can create life even out of death.

Thus, from the experience of meeting Jesus, the disciples could find relatively serviceable images and metaphors in their religious world to express the cause of this meeting. They meet Jesus as a living reality because in fact he does live; and he lives because God has raised him up. In this sense, we might say that the disciples came to proclaim the Resurrection as a causal explanation of their encounter with the living Lord. The experience of the appearances is possible because, unlike other man of the past, Jesus continues to be active in spite of his death. Different as he may appear to be, this activity remains the activity of the same Jesus who was once active on earth. The proclamation of the Resurrection, then, affirms the continued but transformed existence of Jesus after death. From his continued existence flows his continued activity which the disciples experience as a summons to faith and to mission.

To describe the emergence of Easter-faith in this way is not to deny the reality of the glorified Christ, but merely to try to give an historically plausible account of the way the disciples may have come to their surprising conviction without falling into the pitfall of pure subjectivism on the one hand nor into the mistake of crass, materialistic concepts of resurrection on the other. Jesus continues to be active in the lives of the disciples because the God who is the creative source of all life and who can create life even out of death, and who desires to bring all creation to its fulfillment, has done this in Jesus; God has raised him up.

To affirm the Resurrection in this way is understandable historically; that is, if we try to determine the meaning of the texts in relation to the context within which they were written. In such a context, it is thoroughly understandable that there should be a life for Jesus beyond his biological death, for Jewish eschatology and apocalyptic had prepared the ground for this. Yet, the New Testament proclamation makes it clear that the life of the risen Lord is not simply the resuscitation of a corpse nor a return to the condition of history; and thus the Easter proclamation breaks out of the prevalent Old Testament concepts and becomes normative for subsequent Christian eschatology. From this point onward, the Christian hope for the future will never be adequately expressed in terms of programs or projects to be worked out in space and time as we experience it this side of death.

While the approach sketched here may make the emergence of Easter-faith understandable from an historical perspective, it does not prove the truth-value of the Easter-proclamation itself. The argument intends merely to show that it is historically understandable that the disciples should have come to say that Jesus is risen. It cannot go on to prove that the disciples were correct in what they said; for the truth of the Resurrection, in the final analysis, always has been and remains now an issue of faith.

Viewed in this way, the Resurrection is seen as the decisive eschatological act of God's loving, life-giving self-communication to the non-divine. It is, therefore, the decisive act of God's revelation in Jesus, manifesting God to be truly the

God who gives life to the dead (Rom 4: 17); a God whose power extends over life and death; a God whose fidelity and life-giving love have revealed themselves in the new life of the risen Christ. As an eschatological mystery, the Resurrection means that, in Christ, God has accepted the world in mercy, love, and forgiveness with decisiveness. God's final word to his creation is not one of rejection but one of acceptance. Indeed, the Resurrection of Jesus is the decisive beginning of the radical transformation of created reality which will find its fulfillment only when the demands of love have penetrated throughout the world, have transformed the hearts of men and thus have brought about the healing and reconciliation through which God will become all in all and God's love will not be contravened. Hence, the Resurrection of Jesus is not just his private destiny; it is the anticipation of the collective future of mankind. It is the mystery that holds human history open to its future, to the creation of a new mankind and a new world. As the actualization of the full potential of Jesus' humanity, it indicates the full possibilities open to man before God, and thus does not allow us to limit our understanding of life within the confines of what appears possible from a merely human perspective. It allows man to look for no other sort of salvation than that which is indicated in the loving, personal union of Jesus with his Father in the kingdom. Thus, the proclamation of the Resurrection leads theologians today to speak of the "Absolute Future" of man, indicating thereby a future for man with God that cannot be identified with any future that man may create for himself within the space-time framework of his historical existence.

What we have described thus far is, to a great extent, a statement of the content of the original Easter-proclamation as this might be ascertained through historical-critical studies. There remains yet the important question as to whether we today can share this faith. This question is frequently identified with the question of the empty tomb, the third day, or the chemical reconstitution of the corpse of Jesus. If one has problems with any or all of these, he has problems believing in the Resurrection. If one reserves his judgment until such questions are decisively answered, he will hold the possibility of faith in a state of deep-freeze for the whole of his life; for there will very likely be no definitive answers to such problems. This situation has led many theologians to seek some sort of human point of contact for the Christian proclamation. In some way, one seeks, through the application of a phenomenological method, to locate some aspect of human existence to which the inner meaning of the Resurrection can be related. If such a project can be carried out, then it would be possible to speak of sharing the faith of the early disciples even though many questions remain unanswered and will perhaps be forever insoluble.

Such efforts take on various colorations, but in general they work on the assumption that the question of the meaning of human life cannot be answered within history. While man is carried on in life by the question of the final and decisive meaning of his existence, he will really find no answer to the question until he stands at the end of his history. In the mean time, he can only look to his experience in history to see whether there may be any signs pointing in the direction of the meaning he hopes for. On the other side, one can look at the deepest meaning of the Easter-proclamation and find in it a statement about the possibility of human meaning implicit therein.

Thus Rahner writes that to believe in the Resurrection is to believe something about the character of human life and its possibilities; for in its core reality, the Christian faith means to venture the whole of our existence on its being totally directed to God, on its having a meaning, on its being capable of being saved and fulfilled; and on precisely this having occurred in Jesus. Can we believe the same thing of ourselves? We must turn to our own experience and ask what it is we hope for in all the day-to-day projects in which we try to invest our lives with meaning. Do we find ourselves to be incomplete? Do we hope to become better persons? Do we hope to find a fuller life? Do we hope to do something significant with our lives? And if so, what do we think of the constant frustration of our hopes? Above all, what do we think of the death which awaits us all, and which certainly calls into question most radically all that we try to accomplish in life? We think that we are engaged in meaningful work; but in the final analysis, are we really? By questioning ourselves in this way, we may become aware of how profoundly we are incomplete beings who project ourselves in myriad ways to a hoped-for fullness. We begin to see ourselves as hope-filled beings who feel obliged to be faithful to the possibilities of life and yet are constantly threatened by death. In brief, we can begin to see how profoundly we are a question (*Resurrection,* C 2.).

Is there an answer to the question which we are? We can listen to history to ascertain whether there might be an answer. In history we discover many signs pointing in that direction; but on closer analysis, all such signs remain profoundly ambiguous. But in history there are those who claim that the question has an answer, and that the answer is to be found in the Resurrection of Christ. It is an answer that says not only do we seek meaning, but that meaning is possible; not only do we hope, but hope can find fulfillment. It holds out the possibility of fulfillment not in relation to our daily projects, but in relation to our life as such.

Nothing can force us to believe, for faith is always a free response to the God of mystery; and the mystery is never dissolved by rational clarification. At most, such clarification can show that faith is not an immature and irresponsible decision, but can be a decision of intellectual honesty and absolute seriousness. No argument can decisively demonstrate the truth of the Resurrection. But, having discerned its profound significance if it should be taken to be true, we can see the possibility of sharing in the faith of the first disciples in a mature and responsible way. And, since the question that life raises never really disappears, we can ask how else we might come to terms with the question. Are there other options that are genuinely more honest, more mature, and better qualified to enable us to cope with life? Having seen the convergence of a profoundly human question and a truly divine answer in the mystery of Christ, can we not make our own the words of Peter: "Lord, to whom shall we go? You have the message of eternal life" (Jn 6: 68).

CONCLUSION

We speak readily of the text of Scripture as the Word of God, but it is this only in a derived sense. For finally, there is but one Word of God; and that is the act of God in Jesus' humanity, an act that embraces the whole of Jesus' career and that brings that human history to fullness, perfection and completion. All else is either the prerequisite for or the effect of this Word. To hear the Word of God presupposes that we can hear the emptiness, imperfection, and incompleteness of our own existence; for it is at that point that the Word enters most deeply into our lives. To hear our existence is to hear a question to which the Word of God is a response. The response of God is not peripheral, secondary, or external to human existence. Coming from beyond man, it speaks to the very roots of our being, precisely where we hear our existence as most radically contingent and hence as most vulnerable and questionable.

To that question which asks: "What are we to make of the fragile and contingent existence that is ours without our prior consultation?" it answers: "Make yourselves to be freely loving persons, for it is by love that God enters into your lives and rules human affairs. Love is that which transforms men in their personal existence. All genuinely human love is a response to God's love, or it is not human love at all. And all genuine love is accepted by God and is crowned with unending life. This is what you may hope for in your incomplete and fragmented existence." Thus, the Word of God does not speak directly to our categorical hopes, but rather to the hope that springs from the roots of our created being. And as it speaks to that, it sheds light on our day-to-day experience of hope and frustration.

Cross and Resurrection form an indissoluble unity. The cross points to the suffering quality of love and the constant struggle between self-affirmation and self-giving. The cross, however, is a way and not the goal of Christian life. For Christian faith points beyond tragedy to a glory even in the midst of defeat; to hope even as we feel the threat of despair; to a capacity for joy even in days of sorrow; and to life even in death. Thus, viewed from a Christian perspective, there are abundant signs of resurrection-reality coming to us again and again and bringing us constant renewal in moments of decay and defeat. To know this is to know the depths of our existence as a life in God.

The Christian is a man who, like every man, can realistically see all the evidence in experience pointing to meaninglessness and absurdity just as he can see the intimations of meaning; but he places greater weight on the side of meaning. He affirms that behind the apparent confusion and disorder of reality is not simply a blind force, an impersonal fate, nor an empty void, but a living principle of love the clearest expression of which is found in the history of Jesus. What is manifest in Jesus is the basis of universal intelligibility. For man to receive the Word spoken in Jesus is to be liberated from any absolute bond to the finite and to be made free for the mystery of God's love.

For man to hear the Word lived and spoken in Jesus is to hear the deepest truth about reality and about man himself. God is the mystery of love, who takes the risk of creating even when the very creature that emerges may thwart the divine will. Love is that which illumines human existence. This is the style of life toward which man is orientated and without which his existence will be frustrated. The wholeness and completion which man hopes for is grounded in a Love that is stronger than death. Seeing human life from the perspective of Christ, the Christian affirms life over death, sense over non-sense; and he thus looks to the eschatological realization of man's essence in a future with God. And for all this, he makes Eucharist, celebrating the deepest possibilities of life even as he strives to realize them from a sense of fidelity to the mystery of Love from whom he comes and in whom he will find his completion.

Send for complete listing of
all published titles of
SYNTHESIS SERIES

THE SYNTHESIS SERIES

EXISTENTIALISM AND ITS IMPLICATIONS
FOR COUNSELING 75
M. Emmanuel Fontes

A study in depth which leads to seven general principles for integrating existential insights into counseling.

THE CREATION OF FULL HUMAN
PERSONALITY. $1.25
Joseph Drew & William Hague

Complete psychological growth is a process inseparable from total reality—biological and spiritual, internal and external. Vocation is important.

NEW EDUCATIONAL METHODS FOR
INCREASING RELIGIOUS EFFECTIVENESS 75
Dean C. Dauw

Special group methods of self-education that have proved helpful to others are also helpful to religious organizations.

LOVE AND SELFISHNESS 75
Alice von Hildebrand

True love cannot be separated from a joyful readiness to make enduring sacrifices for the sake of the beloved.

A PSYCHOLOGY OF THE CATHOLIC
INTELLECTUAL. 75
Adrian van Kaam

The split between secular and religious learning rooted in psychological history must be healed to prevent disaster.

EMOTIONAL DEVELOPMENT AND SPIRITUAL
GROWTH 75
Timothy J. Gannon

To what extent can insights into a man's emotional life contribute to the solution of problems of spiritual growth.

WHAT'S WRONG WITH GOD .75
Thomas M. Steeman

A probing search into a question that has practical ramifications for the modern man.

HELPING THE DISTURBED RELIGIOUS .75
E.F. Doherty

Like everybody else religious have problems of tensions and anxieties. Their causes and manner of handling are treated with sensitive insight.

WORLD POVERTY ... CAN IT BE SOLVED? .75
Barbara Ward

In depth analysis of the problem of world poverty with sensible suggestions on how to solve it.

A PRIEST FOR ALL SEASONS MASCULINE AND CELIBATE $1.25
Conrad W. Baars, M.D.

Psychiatrist, author, and consultant on the problems of the priesthood at the 1971 Vatican Synod of Bishops, Dr. Baars develops the positive values of celibacy and a regimen to achieve a priesthood both celibate and masculine.

THE RIDDLE OF GENESIS .75
Robert Koch

The study of comparative religion and modern biblical exegesis help to convey the essential message of the first eleven chapters of Genesis.

THE CHURCH TODAY $1.25

Important studies by men like Ratzinger, Schweizer, Congar, Pauwels and Winkhofer on various aspects of the Church in the modern world.

HEDONISM AND EUDEMONISM IN AQUINAS
Thomas A. Mitchell, Ph.D. 2.00

The Thomistic notion of happiness is radically different from both Hedonism and Eudemonism.

HOW TO TREAT AND PREVENT THE CRISIS IN THE PRIESTHOOD $1.25
Conrad Baars, M.D.

A well-known psychiatrist, from vast experiences, discusses the role of the Church in the causation, treatment and prevention of the crisis in the priesthood.

THE MESSAGE OF CHRIST AND THE COUNSELOR $1.50
John Quesnel

An expert discusses the principles of counseling in general and pastoral counseling in particular as gleaned from the life of Christ.

TEMPTATIONS FOR THE THEOLOGY OF LIBERATION .... .75
Bonaventure Kloppenburg O.F.M.

A member of the Papal Theological Commission warns against the various temptations to water down, distort or belittle theology and the Gospel message. A clear voice in babel of confusion.

THE FAMILY PLANNING DILEMMA REVISITED $1.25
John G. Quesnell

Since the publication of **Humane Vitae** a lot of study has been given to family planning. This booklet looks at the new insights in the light of the teaching of the Church. His is an optimistic approach.

RENEWAL AND RECONCILIATION .... .75
Reflections for a Holy Year
Msgr. James O'Reilly

The world, the Church, the family and society plus the sacramental system are discussed within the context of renewal and reconciliation. These reflections are appropriate for any year.

POLITICAL STRUGGLE OF ACTIVE HOMOSEXUALS TO GAIN SOCIAL ACCEPTANCE $1.50
George Kelly

Having learned from civil rights movements, overt homosexuals are exerting strong and expert political pressure to affect public mores.

TO WHOM SHALL WE GO? $1.25
Zachary Hayes O.F.M.

Christ and the mystery of man is the theme of this booklet. It fills a gap as it focuses on the place of Christology in the Church today.

THE MORAL PROBLEM OF CONTRACEPTION .... .75
Msgr. James O'Reilly

This booklet discusses the objective morality, without imputing subjective blame, of the contraceptive act. Contraception is regarded as a devaluation of a basic human good, namely the power to initiate human life.

THE SPIRITUAL DIRECTOR.............. $2.00
Damien Isabell O.F.M.

This is a practical guide for spiritual direction on which growth depends. It contains and overview of approaches and an invaluable bibliography.

THE SACRAMENT OF PENANCE AND RECONCILIATION.................. .75
Msgr. George A. Kelly

This is a sociological and historical study of the changes of attitude and practice of the Sacrament of Reconciliation.

THE HOMOSEXUALS SEARCH FOR HAPPINESS $1.25
Conrad W. Baars, M.D.

In this psycho-philosophical approach Dr. Baars treats homosexuality with remarkable compassion and understanding. He points out that the pressing need is personal, individual affirmation.

AN UNCERTAIN CHURCH
THE NEW CATHOLIC PROBLEM $1.25
George A. Kelly and John A. Flynn

In a clear, concise manner this booklet explores the foundations of academic freedom. It is also a reaffirmation of the great Catholic heritage in intellectual circles.

ROOTS OF HUMAN RIGHTS $2.25
Edward W. O'Rourke, Bishop of Peoria

The most significant events of the past two decades have involved the struggle of individuals and nations for human rights. If the 1980's are to bring a resolution of these struggles, there must be a deeper understanding of human rights.

THE NEED FOR THE MAGISTERIUM
OF THE CHURCH .... .75
K.D. Whitehead

God has established the sacred magisterium in his Church. In a matter as fundamental as our eternal salvation, there has to be a court of appeal to which we have recourse for decisions in answer to the many questions which arise in every age, in every life.

THE UNITY OF THE MORAL
AND THE SPIRITUAL LIFE .... .75
William E. May

The uneasiness many have experienced in integrating their lives as members of a worshipping community with their daily concern and their obligations as parents and citizens is not unresolvable. The moral and spiritual lives are compatible.

THE DIFFERENCE THAT JESUS
MAKES: THE SACRAMENT OF THE
FORGIVING GOD $1.25
Robert Kress

The New Covenant, in the blood of Jesus, is not new in the sense that it existed before. It is new in that it brings to perfection what God has been planning and doing all along—loving, gracing, and living in communion with human beings.

THE NATURE AND MEANING OF CHASTITY $1.25
William E. May, Ph.D.

Chastity is a loving integration of sex and affection into our lives enabling us, as sexual beings, to love and be loved. This definition is explained in detail.

LAY AND RELIGIOUS STATES OF LIFE: THEIR DISTINCTION AND COMPLEMENTARITY .... .75
James O'Reilly

The distinction between the lay and religious states of life must be maintained because of the nature of the movement of man toward salvation and the effect of the environment of life in the world.

THE PASCHAL MYSTERY: CORE GRACE IN THE LIFE OF THE CHRISTIAN .... .75
Augustine Paul Hennesy C.P.

Christian hope lies in the Risen Christ. Christians must learn to take on Christ's attitude toward the cross and the glory of it.

VALUING SUFFERING AS A CHRISTIAN: SOME PSYCHOLOGICAL PERSPECTIVES .... .75
Henry C. Simmons C.P.

Within the mystery of the cross of Christ, the sufferings of daily life hold meaning and value. Christian hope lies in the promises of Christ's death and resurrection.

SEX, LOVE AND PROCREATION .... .75
William E. May

This booklet is concerned with the important question: Can sexual intercourse as an act of love ever be separated from intercourse as a creative act?

CONTEMPORARY CULTURE AND CHRISTIANITY $1.50
Maurice DeLange

A man-centered society is usually tempted to say that the ultimate meaning in life is absurdity and nothingness. A god-centered society, wherein love is shared with fellow men and women, can indeed show the real meaning of life.

THE QUEST FOR SECURITY $3.50
Alfred Martin O.F.M.

Every age has its own panacea. In our time it is a quest for security. We all want security of all kinds—economic, social, material, mental. But security is a state of mind with religion as an essential element.

MENTAL HEALTH: PSYCHOTHERAPY OF TOMORROW $2.50
Alfred Martin O.F.M.

Because there is an intimate relationship between body and soul, what affects one will affect the other. This mutual influence has a pervading effect on mental health.

MINISTRY TO THE SICK AND DYING:
The Pastoral Reflection Paper............... $1.75
(Washington Theological Union)
Jude J. McGeehan O.F.M.

Christ is the Divine Physician of mankind . . . Because sickness cannot be separated from its religious import in the history of salvation, the Apostolate to the Sick is one of the most essential missions of the Church.

MINIMUM ORDER $5.00

Synthesis Series is published by
FRANCISCAN HERALD PRESS
1434 WEST 51st STREET
CHICAGO, ILLINOIS 60609